TO:

_____

FROM:

_____

BUDDHISM FOR YOU

Love

BUDDHISM FOR YOU

Love

DAISAKU IKEDA

MIDDLEWAY
PRESS

Published by Middleway Press
A division of the SGI-USA
606 Wilshire Blvd., Santa Monica, CA 90401

Design by Lightbourne, Inc.

Printed in Korea

10 9 8 7 6 5

Library of Congress Cataloging-in-Publication Data

Ikeda, Daisaku.
    Buddhism for you. Love / Daisaku Ikeda.
        p. cm.

    ISBN-13: 978-0-9723267-7-3 (hardcover : alk. paper)
    I. Religious life--Soka Gakkai. 2. Love--Religious aspects--
Buddhism. I. Title.
BQ8499.I384B833   2006
294.3'5696--dc22

                            2006028526

ISBN: 978-0-9723267-7-3

*T*rue love arises
from two people's determination
to share their lives together,
and from the wisdom gained from
aspiring for the future.

*I*t is important to love people,
to treasure everyone. To the extent that
we love others, we will be loved. To the extent
that we work for others' happiness, we will enjoy
protection and support. This is the law
of cause and effect. It is also the path
for developing our humanity.

If you genuinely love someone,
then through your relationship
with him or her, you can develop into
a person whose love extends to all humanity.
That sort of relationship strengthens
and enriches your inner realm.

The ideal love is the one that enables
each of the lovers to influence and enhance
the other's personality.

—*Josei Toda*

Ideal love is fostered only between
two sincere, mature and independent people.
It is essential, therefore, that you make
polishing yourself a priority and do not
get carried away by romance.

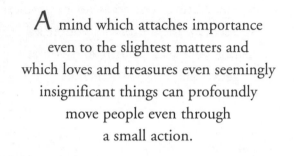

A mind which attaches importance
even to the slightest matters and
which loves and treasures even seemingly
insignificant things can profoundly
move people even through
a small action.

4

Rather than becoming so love-struck
that you create a world where only
the two of you exist, it is much healthier
to learn from those aspects of your partner
that you respect and admire and
continue to make efforts to improve
and develop yourself.

At what time, what moment, should we ever allow ourselves to forget the compassionate vow of the Buddha, who declared, "At all times I think to myself: [How can I cause living beings to gain entry into the unsurpassed way and quickly acquire the body of a Buddha]?"

—*Nichiren*

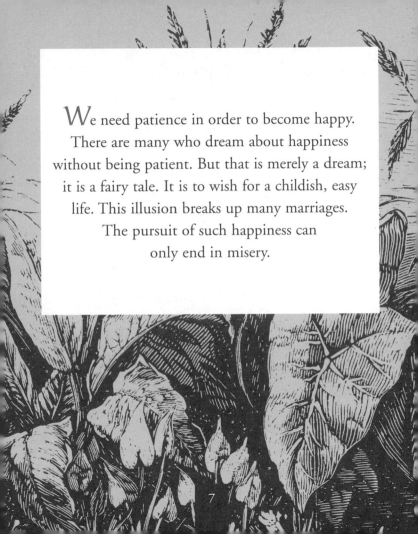

We need patience in order to become happy.
There are many who dream about happiness
without being patient. But that is merely a dream;
it is a fairy tale. It is to wish for a childish, easy
life. This illusion breaks up many marriages.
The pursuit of such happiness can
only end in misery.

It is important for a couple to listen to each other.
Men in particular should listen to what women
have to say. It is also important for a couple
to compliment and praise each other.
It could be for anything—praising one another
is what matters. Nothing comes from
pointing out the other person's faults.
That's just foolishness.

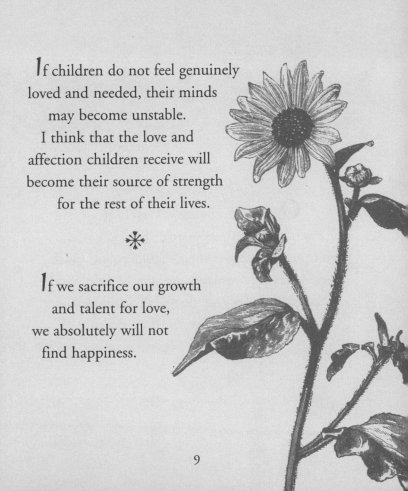

If children do not feel genuinely
loved and needed, their minds
may become unstable.
I think that the love and
affection children receive will
become their source of strength
for the rest of their lives.

❈

If we sacrifice our growth
and talent for love,
we absolutely will not
find happiness.

9

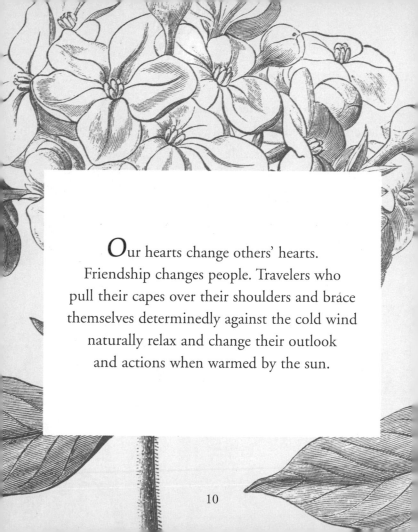

Our hearts change others' hearts. Friendship changes people. Travelers who pull their capes over their shoulders and brace themselves determinedly against the cold wind naturally relax and change their outlook and actions when warmed by the sun.

If we believe in Nam-myoho-renge-kyo,
then we can be together with our loved ones in
lifetime after lifetime. Sometimes we may be
related as parent and child, other times as
husband and wife, other times as siblings
or close friends. While the relationships
may take various forms, we can be
confident that we will be born near
each other again and again.

11

If human relationships are based on the idea
of reward, with the feeling that "I have done
this much for this person, so I expect him
to do the same for me," then this kind
of relationship can only be fragile.

People who respect others are respected
by others in return. Those who are unstinting
in their compassion and concern for others
are also protected and supported by others.
Our environment is essentially a
reflection of ourselves.

Tall trees grow from secure and solid ground.
Please give your children a home where
they can enjoy tranquility
and peace of mind.

Buddhists always give the greatest thought
and effort to how and what they themselves
can do to steer everything in the direction
of harmony and joy—to enable everyone
to enjoy themselves and be happy.

*T*he ideal relationship is one in which
you mutually aim at a great future goal,
encouraging and helping
each other develop.

*P*eace exists in the hearts of people
who love children.

There are many people, many lives,
on this planet, too numerous, in fact, to count.
From this great multitude, we wondrously find
ourselves together with those in our families—
as parents and children, as brothers and sisters,
as husbands and wives. If we do not live
joyfully and cheerfully in the company of
those with whom we share
this profound bond,
what is life for?

We should give first priority to the development of an independent spirit as a human being before considering one's role as a man, woman, child or parent. In other words, in order for a person to become a man, woman, child or parent in the true sense of the word, one has to first of all develop his or her autonomous identity as a human being.

There are many reasons why people bid farewell to one another. It may be difficult indeed not to look back. Yet you have to advance, even a step. As long as you advance, new hope will be born. The sun will rise. A new life will unfold for you.

The love between husband and wife
or parent and child is an expression
of unadorned humanity,
of the pure human heart.

Consideration equals strength,
so the more considerate of others you are,
the stronger you will become.

Whether people get divorced or not,
the important thing is that they become happy.
Whether someone is married or not, has
children or not, of utmost importance is happiness.
This is what faith is about. For happiness
exists within our own life.

How can we cause the immense love
and compassion of the original Buddha to
rain down upon the entire world? This is the
thought that constantly occupies my mind;
this is my constant determination.

When a couple has shared the joys and sorrows
of life over a long period of time, a deep tie
grows up between them and it cannot
be severed by any outside force.

Parents' spontaneous smiles and their
unaffected bearing filter through the hearts
of children like a shaft of bright light coming
through the window of a dark room or
the fragrance of flowers scenting
the surrounding air.

The love of parents showered upon
the lives of young people will become their
sustenance for their whole lives.

Even though we strive to treat everyone
with love and compassion, since we are
ordinary people, it is only natural that
we will have likes and dislikes. There is no
need for us to struggle to make ourselves fond
of people we find disagreeable. In our work
as emissaries of the Buddha, we must not let
our thoughts or actions be colored by
any discrimination or favoritism.

A mother's love is unimaginably deep
and her influence profound. If all people treasured
their mothers, the world would undoubtedly
be filled with peace and happiness.
Love and peace are the
lifeblood of a home.

In a relationship, it is demeaning to constantly
seek your partner's approval. In such relationships
real caring, depth or even love is missing.
If you are not treated the way your heart says
you should be, I hope you will have the courage
and dignity to decide that you are better off
risking your partner's scorn than
enduring unhappiness.

Love is not two people gazing at each other,
but two people looking ahead together
in the same direction.

—*Antoine de Saint-Exupéry*

A married life that proceeds smoothly
and without difficulty, more or less by force
of habit, may appear to be a happy one; in
many cases it is not in fact happy at all.
The important thing is not to escape trouble
and hardship, but when it comes, to know
how to face it without grumblings
and mutual incriminations.

Those who make many friends
have greater opportunities for
growth and self-development;
they make society a better place
and lead happy, satisfying lives.

The compassion, love and courage
of parents are the greatest
marks of humanity.

Relationship problems are opportunities
to grow and mature. Such problems can be
character building if you don't let them defeat you.
That's why it's important not to isolate yourself.
No one can exist apart from others. Remaining
aloof from others cultivates selfishness,
which accomplishes nothing.

The genuine love of a father consists in wholeheartedly doing anything for the sake of his children. Children who have such a father are fortunate. I believe it is an important mission for a father to powerfully support his children, especially when they are standing at an important crossroads.

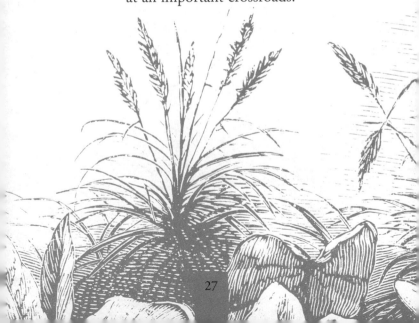

Nichiren writes, "If you light a lantern for another, it will also brighten your own way." Please be confident that the higher your flame of altruistic action burns, the more its light will suffuse your life with happiness. Those who possess an altruistic spirit are the happiest people of all.

When you are sincere in consideration
for others, in even the most trifling matters,
then you can bring about a complete change
in the world around you.

Even if it's only a brief meeting, give your children
a hug when you see them. Touch them and talk
to them. Try to make time to listen to what they
have to say. As long as you have love and
compassion, you will find the wisdom
to make this work.

In life we will encounter separations of inexpressible sadness. However, those who overcome such grief and continue to live with strength and courage will be cherished and respected by their juniors as kings and queens of life.

I wish to protect and encourage all parents and children, and I will do whatever I can for their sake. To protect parents and children is to protect life itself; it is to nurture peace and protect the future.

Even if someone is close by, their heart
may be distant. But if someone is far away,
if there is a heart-to-heart bond, they could not
be closer. The heart is what counts. In the
world of the heart, there is
no separation.

32

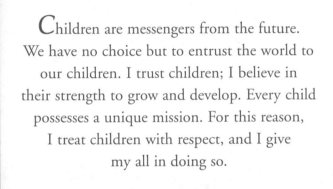

Children are messengers from the future.
We have no choice but to entrust the world to
our children. I trust children; I believe in
their strength to grow and develop. Every child
possesses a unique mission. For this reason,
I treat children with respect, and I give
my all in doing so.

33

Having good friends is like being equipped with a powerful auxiliary engine. When we encounter a steep hill or an obstacle, we can encourage one another and find the strength to keep pressing forward vigorously.

A shallow person will have only shallow
relationships. Real love is not one person
clinging to another; it can only be fostered
between two strong people secure
in their individuality.

Let those who love what is right join hands,
and let us have but one banner—
the banner of action and virtue.

—*Leo Tolstoy*

Buddhism teaches that the altruistic way
of life glows with the flame of wisdom.
The bodhisattva way is to let wisdom put
knowledge to use and to couple compassion
with compassionate action.

Human life is not a sad affair. In all things
use your intellect and power of reason.
Let your life be imbued with feelings
that are based on pure love.

—*Josei Toda*

The love between husband and wife becomes more mature when the initial passion is elevated through wisdom to encompass spiritual love and humanistic compassion. By so doing, the couple is able to walk along the tree-lined avenue of life hand in hand, enjoying the soft breeze of happiness.

By expanding their love from the personal to the universal level, women can become a great force against war and for peace.

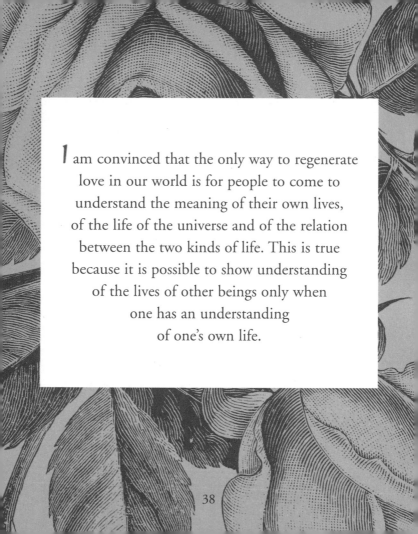

I am convinced that the only way to regenerate
love in our world is for people to come to
understand the meaning of their own lives,
of the life of the universe and of the relation
between the two kinds of life. This is true
because it is possible to show understanding
of the lives of other beings only when
one has an understanding
of one's own life.

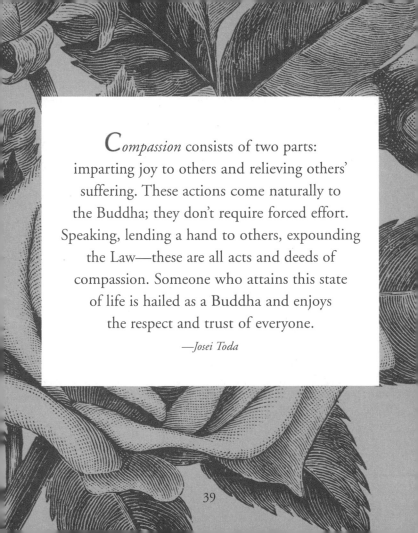

Compassion consists of two parts:
imparting joy to others and relieving others'
suffering. These actions come naturally to
the Buddha; they don't require forced effort.
Speaking, lending a hand to others, expounding
the Law—these are all acts and deeds of
compassion. Someone who attains this state
of life is hailed as a Buddha and enjoys
the respect and trust of everyone.

—*Josei Toda*

If you have wisdom alone and lack compassion, it will be a cold, perverse wisdom. If you have compassion alone and lack wisdom, you cannot give happiness to others. You are even likely to lead them in the wrong direction, and you won't be able to achieve your own happiness.

If you are neglecting things you should be doing, forgetting your purpose in life because of the relationship you're in, then you're on the wrong path.

I ask parents to pour love upon their children like the sun nurturing sunflowers. This is because people can live powerfully for the rest of their lives with the energy of love that they received in their childhood.

More valuable than treasures in a storehouse are the treasures of the body, and the treasures of the heart are the most valuable of all. From the time you read this letter on, strive to accumulate the treasures of the heart!

—*Nichiren*

If you use love as an escape, the euphoria
is unlikely to last long. However much we
may try, we can never run away from ourselves.
We will never find happiness if we don't
change ourselves from within.

Even married people
were once strangers.
Without patience and
the effort to understand
one another, things are
not likely to go well.
Patience is necessary
for a couple to live together,
earn a living, protect their home
and educate their children
while dedicating themselves
for the sake of others.

The important thing is to overcome the sorrow
that accompanies any type of separation,
such as death or divorce. The vital thing
is to continue advancing.
Do not look back.

For the sake
of these living beings/
I summon up a mind
of great compassion.

—*The Lotus Sutra*

*T*ruly praiseworthy are those who have a sense of gratitude and appreciation toward their parents. The Buddhist sutras teach that the practice of Buddhism is the ultimate expression of devotion to one's parents, and the Buddha excels in such dedication and concern.

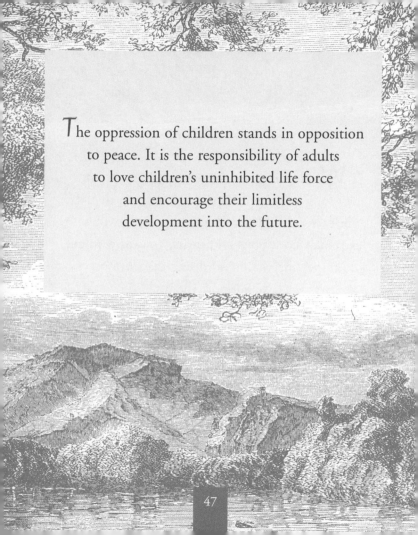

The oppression of children stands in opposition
to peace. It is the responsibility of adults
to love children's uninhibited life force
and encourage their limitless
development into the future.

47

Without respect, no relationship will last very long nor can two people bring out the best in each other. I personally hope men will be extremely courteous and caring toward women, respecting them and doing their utmost to support them.

The Buddha transmits the heart's sunlight universally to all beings.

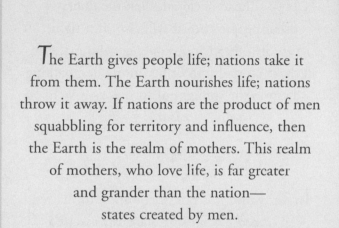

The Earth gives people life; nations take it from them. The Earth nourishes life; nations throw it away. If nations are the product of men squabbling for territory and influence, then the Earth is the realm of mothers. This realm of mothers, who love life, is far greater and grander than the nation—states created by men.

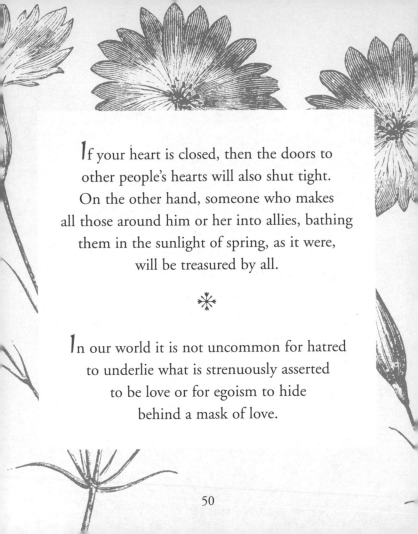

If your heart is closed, then the doors to
other people's hearts will also shut tight.
On the other hand, someone who makes
all those around him or her into allies, bathing
them in the sunlight of spring, as it were,
will be treasured by all.

❄

In our world it is not uncommon for hatred
to underlie what is strenuously asserted
to be love or for egoism to hide
behind a mask of love.

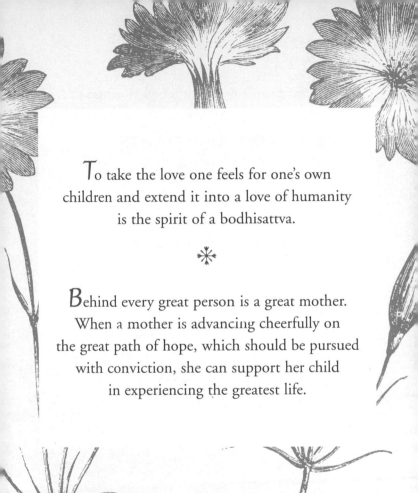

*T*o take the love one feels for one's own
children and extend it into a love of humanity
is the spirit of a bodhisattva.

❄

*B*ehind every great person is a great mother.
When a mother is advancing cheerfully on
the great path of hope, which should be pursued
with conviction, she can support her child
in experiencing the greatest life.

Great people never forget what others
have done for them. In fact, having a sense
of appreciation makes a person
worthy of respect.

What is friendship? True friendship implies
a relationship where you empathize with your
friends when they're suffering and encourage
them not to lose heart, and where they,
in turn, empathize with you when you're
in the same situation and try
to cheer you up.

Compassion is not a Buddhist austerity.
It is something that should be expressed
unconsciously and naturally in one's actions,
and in the workings of one's heart. The Buddha
knows no path of living apart from that of
living with compassion.

—*Josei Toda*

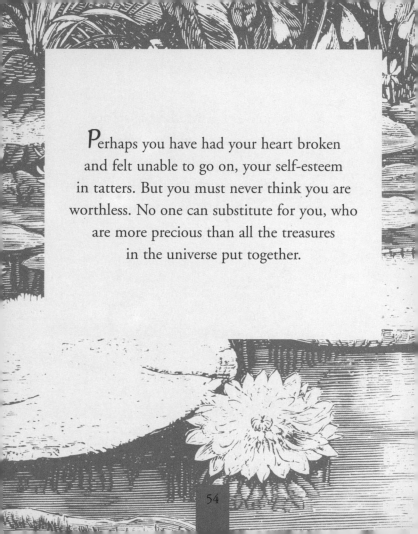

Perhaps you have had your heart broken
and felt unable to go on, your self-esteem
in tatters. But you must never think you are
worthless. No one can substitute for you, who
are more precious than all the treasures
in the universe put together.

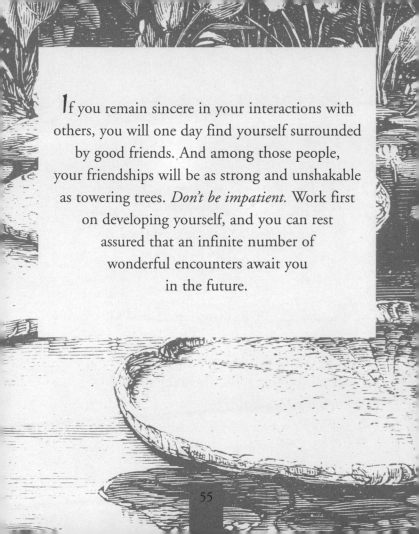

If you remain sincere in your interactions with others, you will one day find yourself surrounded by good friends. And among those people, your friendships will be as strong and unshakable as towering trees. *Don't be impatient.* Work first on developing yourself, and you can rest assured that an infinite number of wonderful encounters await you in the future.

The only way to fulfill the potential
of the human race is to live just, kind,
benevolent and compassionate lives.

Mutual respect and trust are crucial for creating
real friendship. Naturally, there will be times
when you have arguments and disagreements
with your friends. But there should always be an
underlying spirit of respect and consideration
for each other. In friendship, we mustn't
think only of ourselves.

The most attractive person is one who can continue
to make steady efforts to fulfill his or her dream
even if others do not recognize
their dedication.

The flame of faith breaks through our tiny,
confined state of life in which we are preoccupied
solely with our own concerns and welfare.
Our friends' victories become our victories,
and our victories become theirs.

*Additional books in this series
are available and include:*

Courage
Determination
Prayer

To order please visit:
www.MiddlewayPress.com

*For more information about the SGI,
please visit:* www.sgi-usa.org